WELCOME TO THE U.S.A.
WEST VIRGINIA

Written by Ann Heinrichs   Illustrated by Matt Kania
Content Adviser: Paul Rakes, PhD, Assistant Professor,
History Department, West Virginia University of Technology,
Montgomery, West Virginia

The Child's World®

Published in the United States of America by The Child's World®
PO Box 326 • Chanhassen, MN 55317-0326
800-599-READ • www.childsworld.com

Photo Credits
Cover: David Muench/Corbis; frontispiece: Getty Images/Taxi/Richard Nowitz.

Interior: Corbis: 14 (Mark E. Gibson), 26 (Reuters), 30 (Peter Harholdt), 33 (James L. Amos); David Fattaleh/WV Tourism: 6, 21, 25, 29; Michael Keller/West Virginia Division of Culture and History: 10; Library of Congress: 15; Jack Mills/West Virginia State Wildlife Center: 9; Mountain State Forest Festival: 22; Steve Shaluta/WV Tourism: 13, 17, 34; West Virginia Italian Heritage Festival: 18.

Acknowledgments
The Child's World®: Mary Berendes, Publishing Director

Editorial Directions, Inc.: E. Russell Primm, Editorial Director; Katie Marsico, Associate Editor; Judith Shiffer, Assistant Editor; Matt Messbarger, Editorial Assistant; Susan Hindman, Copy Editor; Melissa McDaniel, Proofreader; Kevin Cunningham, Peter Garnham, Matt Messbarger, Olivia Nellums, Chris Simms, Molly Symmonds, Katherine Trickle, Carl Stephen Wender, Fact Checkers; Tim Griffin/IndexServ, Indexer; Cian Loughlin O'Day, Photo Researcher and Editor

The Design Lab: Kathleen Petelinsek, Design; Julia Goozen, Art Production

Library of Congress Cataloging-in-Publication Data
Heinrichs, Ann.
  West Virginia / by Ann Heinrichs ; cartography and illustrations by Matt Kania.
    p. cm. — (Welcome to the U.S.A.)
  Includes index.
  ISBN 1-59296-490-7 (library bound : alk. paper)
  1. West Virginia—Juvenile literature. I. Kania, Matt, ill. II. Title.
  F241.3.H453 2006
  975.4—dc22   2005004815

About the Author
Ann Heinrichs

Ann Heinrichs is the author of more than 100 books for children and young adults. She has also enjoyed successful careers as a children's book editor and an advertising copywriter. Ann grew up in Fort Smith, Arkansas, and lives in Chicago, Illinois.

About the Map Illustrator
Matt Kania

Matt Kania loves maps and, as a kid, dreamed of making them. In school he studied geography and cartography, and today he makes maps for a living. Matt's favorite thing about drawing maps is learning about the places they represent. Many of the maps he has created can be found in books, magazines, videos, Web sites, and public places.

On the cover: Hang out with the birds high above New River Gorge!
On page one: Ride into Charleston for a taste of city life!

OUR WEST VIRGINIA TRIP

L et's take a trip through West Virginia! You'll find it's a great place to explore.

You'll hike up mountains and wander through forests. You'll go deep down into a coal mine. You'll hear fiddlers and visit logging camps. You'll see a gigantic radio telescope. You'll watch glassblowers make glass. And you'll eat all the pasta you can hold!

How's that for a fun trip? Are you ready to roll? Then buckle up and hang on tight. It's time to hit the road!

WELCOME TO WEST VIRGINIA

As you travel through West Virginia, watch for all the interesting facts along the way.

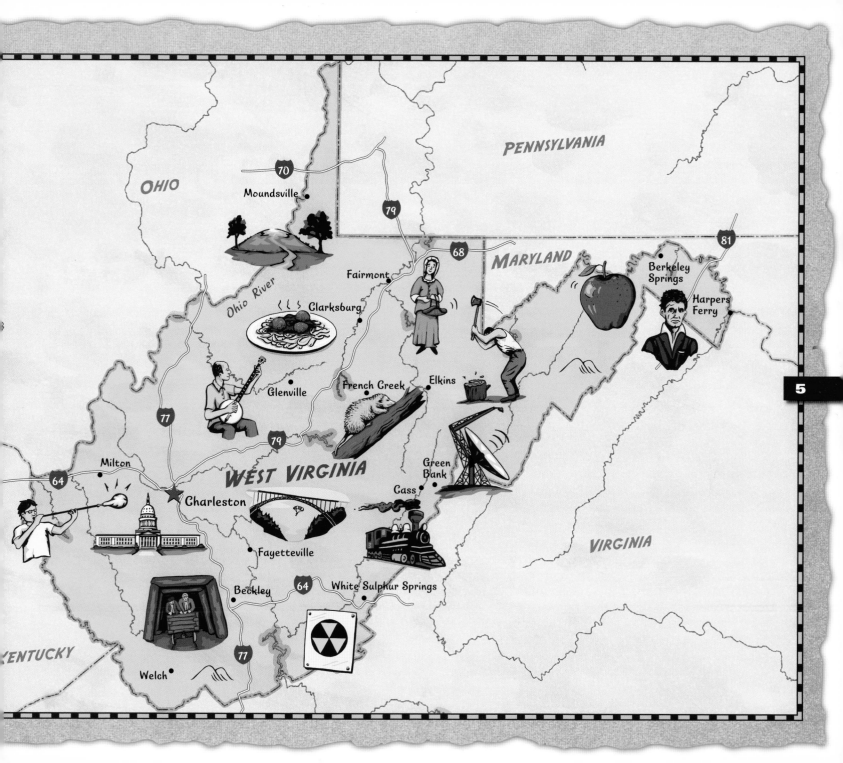

OHIO

PENNSYLVANIA

MARYLAND

VIRGINIA

KENTUCKY

WEST VIRGINIA

70

79

68

81

77

79

64

64

77

Moundsville

Ohio River

Fairmont

Clarksburg

Glenville

French Creek

Elkins

Berkeley Springs

Harpers Ferry

Milton

Charleston

Green Bank

Cass

Fayetteville

Beckley

White Sulphur Springs

Welch

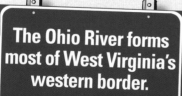

Hang on tight! Parachutists soar over New River Gorge on Bridge Day.

The Ohio River forms most of West Virginia's western border.

Bridge Day at New River Gorge

Stand high on the bridge. Look down, and there's a river far below. You're probably gripping tightly to the railing. But dozens of people are leaping off the bridge!

What's going on here? It's Bridge Day in Fayetteville's New River Gorge! People parachute or **rappel** to the bottom. Not just anyone can do it, though. The jumpers have to be experts.

The New River cuts through the mountains. Mountains cover much of West Virginia. The Appalachian Mountains are in the east. The Allegheny Mountains are part of this area. To the west are steep hills and valleys. Many rivers and streams rush through the mountains.

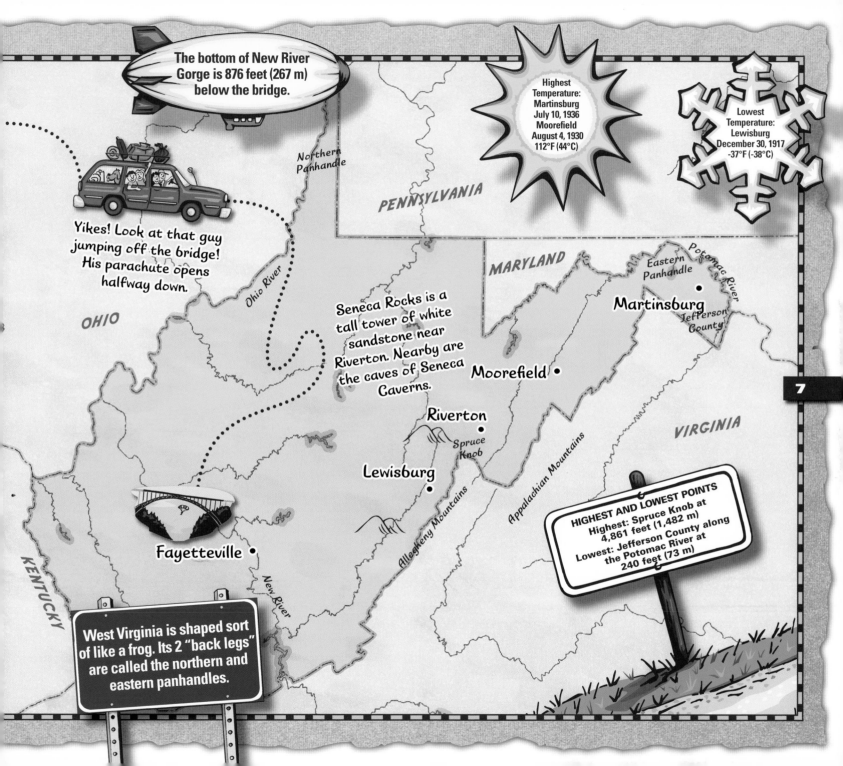

The bottom of New River Gorge is 876 feet (267 m) below the bridge.

Highest Temperature: Martinsburg July 10, 1936 Moorefield August 4, 1930 112°F (44°C)

Lowest Temperature: Lewisburg December 30, 1917 -37°F (-38°C)

Yikes! Look at that guy jumping off the bridge! His parachute opens halfway down.

Northern Panhandle

PENNSYLVANIA

MARYLAND

Eastern Panhandle

Potomac River

Ohio River

OHIO

Seneca Rocks is a tall tower of white sandstone near Riverton. Nearby are the caves of Seneca Caverns.

Martinsburg

Jefferson County

Moorefield

Riverton

Spruce Knob

VIRGINIA

Lewisburg

Appalachian Mountains

Allegheny Mountains

HIGHEST AND LOWEST POINTS
Highest: Spruce Knob at 4,861 feet (1,482 m)
Lowest: Jefferson County along the Potomac River at 240 feet (73 m)

Fayetteville

KENTUCKY

New River

West Virginia is shaped sort of like a frog. Its 2 "back legs" are called the northern and eastern panhandles.

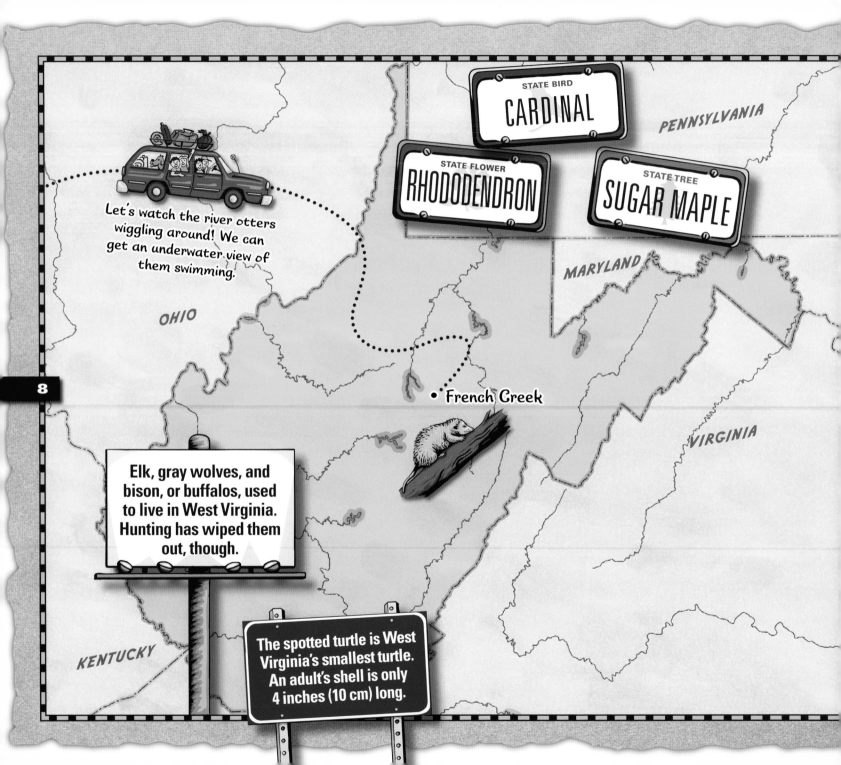

STATE BIRD
CARDINAL

STATE FLOWER
RHODODENDRON

STATE TREE
SUGAR MAPLE

PENNSYLVANIA

MARYLAND

OHIO

Let's watch the river otters wiggling around! We can get an underwater view of them swimming.

• French Creek

VIRGINIA

Elk, gray wolves, and bison, or buffalos, used to live in West Virginia. Hunting has wiped them out, though.

KENTUCKY

The spotted turtle is West Virginia's smallest turtle. An adult's shell is only 4 inches (10 cm) long.

8

The Wildlife Center in French Creek

Wander along the wooded trails. Suddenly, you're face to face with a bear!

Are you deep in the wilderness? In a way, you are. You're visiting the West Virginia State Wildlife Center. Its forests are full of wildlife. Bears, bobcats, and many other animals roam here. But fences separate the animals from human visitors!

Forests cover most of West Virginia. They make a great home for wild animals. Deer and bears live there. So do foxes, skunks, and raccoons. Chipmunks and rabbits scurry through the leaves. They're looking for nuts, grains, or berries.

These elk call French Creek home.

The National Park Service has 6 sites in West Virginia.

Grave Creek Mound dates back thousands of years.

It looks like a cone-shaped mountain. But people built this giant mound. It's Grave Creek Mound in Moundsville. The Adena people built it about 2,000 years ago. They piled up tons of earth. They buried many of their dead inside.

Several Native American groups arrived after the Adena. Some were farmers, and others were hunters. In the 1600s, the Iroquois became very powerful. They tried to control the area. They wanted to hunt fur-bearing animals there. They traded the furs to Europeans.

White settlers arrived in about 1730. At this point, some Indian groups still lived in the area.

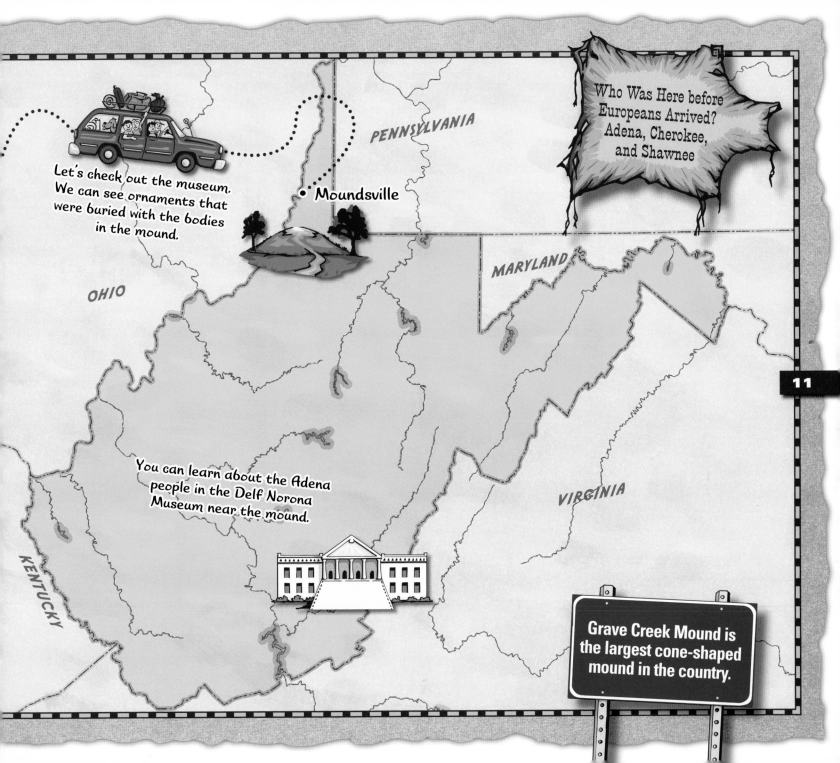

Let's check out the museum. We can see ornaments that were buried with the bodies in the mound.

PENNSYLVANIA

• Moundsville

Who Was Here before Europeans Arrived? Adena, Cherokee, and Shawnee

MARYLAND

OHIO

You can learn about the Adena people in the Delf Norona Museum near the mound.

VIRGINIA

KENTUCKY

Grave Creek Mound is the largest cone-shaped mound in the country.

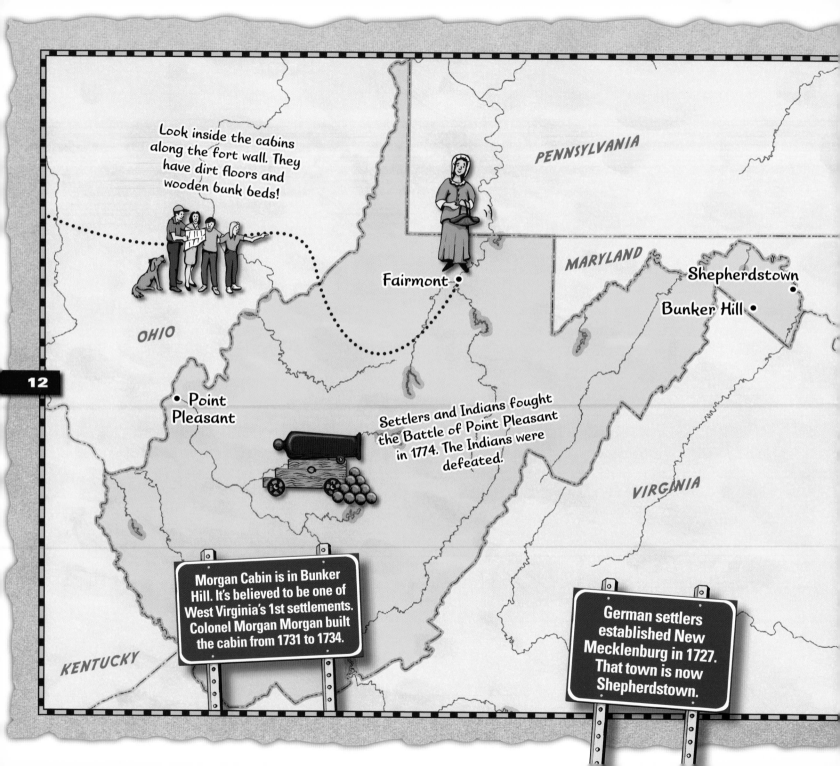

Look inside the cabins along the fort wall. They have dirt floors and wooden bunk beds!

PENNSYLVANIA

MARYLAND

Shepherdstown •

Bunker Hill •

Fairmont •

OHIO

• Point Pleasant

Settlers and Indians fought the Battle of Point Pleasant in 1774. The Indians were defeated!

VIRGINIA

Morgan Cabin is in Bunker Hill. It's believed to be one of West Virginia's 1st settlements. Colonel Morgan Morgan built the cabin from 1731 to 1734.

German settlers established New Mecklenburg in 1727. That town is now Shepherdstown.

KENTUCKY

Prickett's Fort near Fairmont

Step back in history at Prickett's Fort! People are spinning yarn and weaving cloth. Some are cooking in big kettles. There are blacksmiths and gunmakers, too.

This fort was first built in the 1700s. Now costumed workers are busy there. They show you how West Virginia **pioneers** lived.

English settlers established the Virginia **Colony** in 1607. It included land that is now West Virginia. At first, no settlers moved that far west. Pioneers first came in the 1700s.

Most pioneers lived as farmers. They often clashed with Indians in the area. Many forts were set up to protect settlers. One was Prickett's Fort. Settlers gathered inside for safety.

Are you back in the 1700s? A costumed craft worker fashions a gun at Prickett's Fort.

John Brown's raid on Harpers Ferry began on October 16, 1859.

John Brown raided this government arsenal in 1859.

West Virginia was the 35th state to enter the Union. It joined on June 20, 1863.

Harpers Ferry and the Civil War

John Brown had a plan. One night in 1859, he sneaked into Harpers Ferry. There he raided a government **arsenal.** He hoped to steal thousands of guns. He wanted to use them to free the slaves. Brown's plan failed. He was caught and hanged. But his raid stirred up people's feelings. It helped lead to the Civil War (1861–1865).

The states fought this war over slavery. The Northern, or Union, side opposed slavery. Southern, or Confederate, states wanted to keep slavery.

Virginia joined the Confederacy. But many western Virginians opposed slavery. They formed the state of West Virginia and joined the Union. The Union won the war.

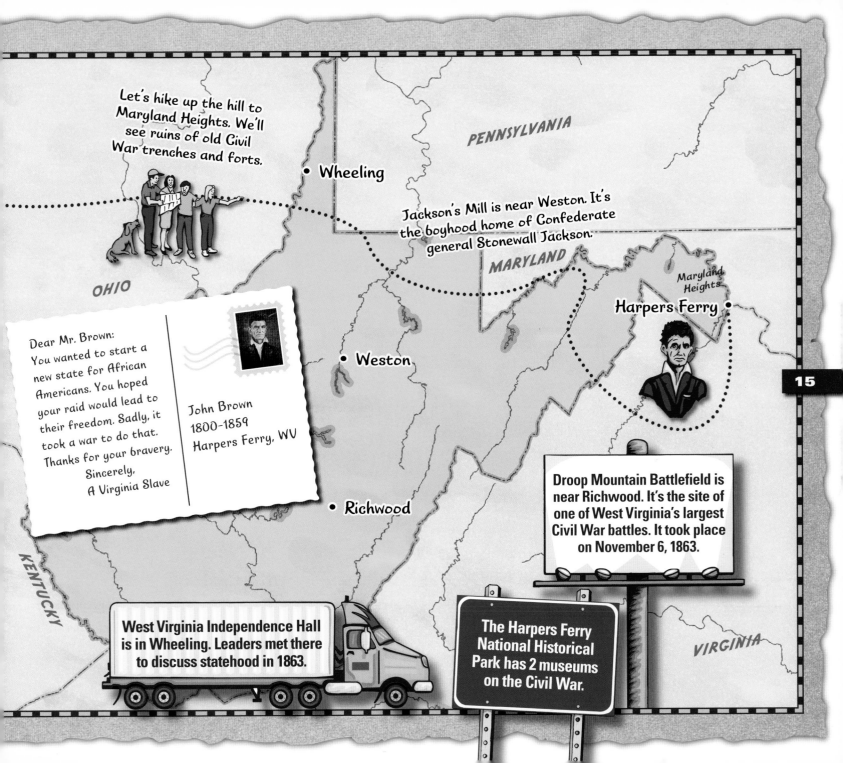

Let's hike up the hill to Maryland Heights. We'll see ruins of old Civil War trenches and forts.

PENNSYLVANIA

• Wheeling

Jackson's Mill is near Weston. It's the boyhood home of Confederate general Stonewall Jackson.

MARYLAND

Maryland Heights

Harpers Ferry

OHIO

Dear Mr. Brown:
You wanted to start a new state for African Americans. You hoped your raid would lead to their freedom. Sadly, it took a war to do that. Thanks for your bravery.
Sincerely,
A Virginia Slave

John Brown
1800-1859
Harpers Ferry, WV

• Weston

• Richwood

Droop Mountain Battlefield is near Richwood. It's the site of one of West Virginia's largest Civil War battles. It took place on November 6, 1863.

KENTUCKY

West Virginia Independence Hall is in Wheeling. Leaders met there to discuss statehood in 1863.

The Harpers Ferry National Historical Park has 2 museums on the Civil War.

VIRGINIA

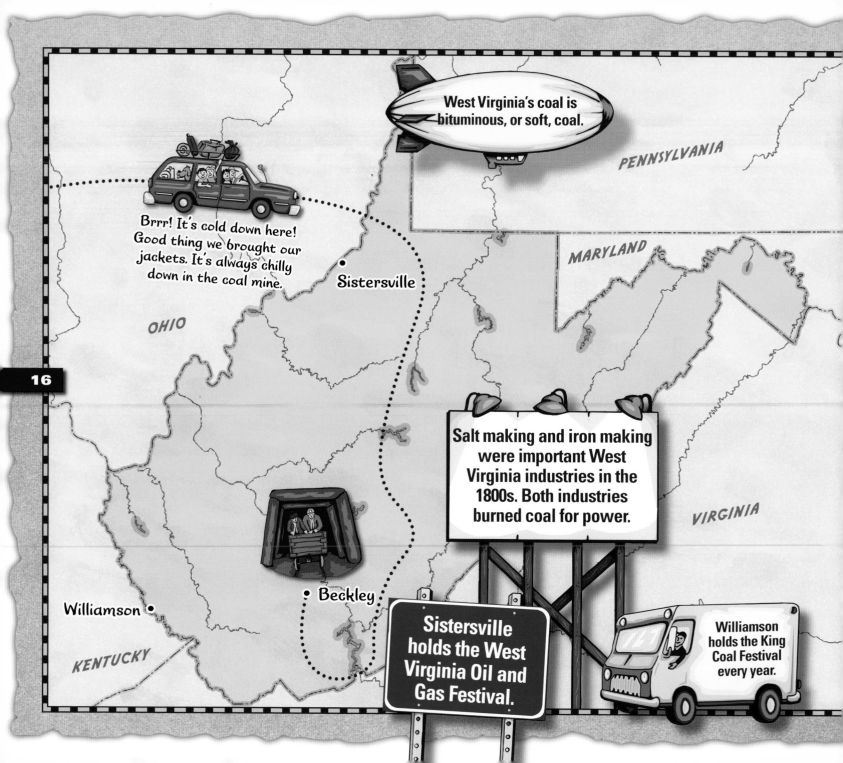

West Virginia's coal is bituminous, or soft, coal.

PENNSYLVANIA

Brrr! It's cold down here! Good thing we brought our jackets. It's always chilly down in the coal mine.

Sistersville

OHIO

MARYLAND

Salt making and iron making were important West Virginia industries in the 1800s. Both industries burned coal for power.

VIRGINIA

Beckley

Williamson

KENTUCKY

Sistersville holds the West Virginia Oil and Gas Festival.

Williamson holds the King Coal Festival every year.

Beckley Exhibition Coal Mine

Climb into the creaky train car. You're heading deep underground. There you'll wind through dark, black tunnels.

You're exploring Beckley Exhibition Coal Mine. And your guide is a real coal miner. He explains how miners used to work there.

Most parts of West Virginia contain coal. The mineral was first discovered there in 1742. Thousands of miners were working by the 1890s. They mined the coal with picks and shovels. It was dirty and dangerous work. Sometimes miners died in mine explosions.

By 1900, coal mining was the state's biggest **industry.** Coal helped other industries, too. Factories burned the coal in their furnaces.

Would you make a good miner? Tour Beckley Exhibition Coal Mine and find out!

Beckley Exhibition Coal Mine goes down 1,500 feet (450 m) underground.

Stop by Clarksburg's Italian Heritage Festival. It's filled with food, games, and even a royal court!

Do you like pasta? Want to enter a hot-pepper-eating contest? Then come to the Italian Heritage Festival! You'll be swept up in lively Italian music. And you'll eat your fill of Italian food!

Italians are among West Virginia's many **ethnic** groups. Many Italians arrived in the late 1800s. They came to work in the coal mines.

Other **immigrants** came from Poland, Germany, or Hungary. Some worked in the coal and lumber industries. Others worked in factories. Many groups still celebrate their **cultures** today.

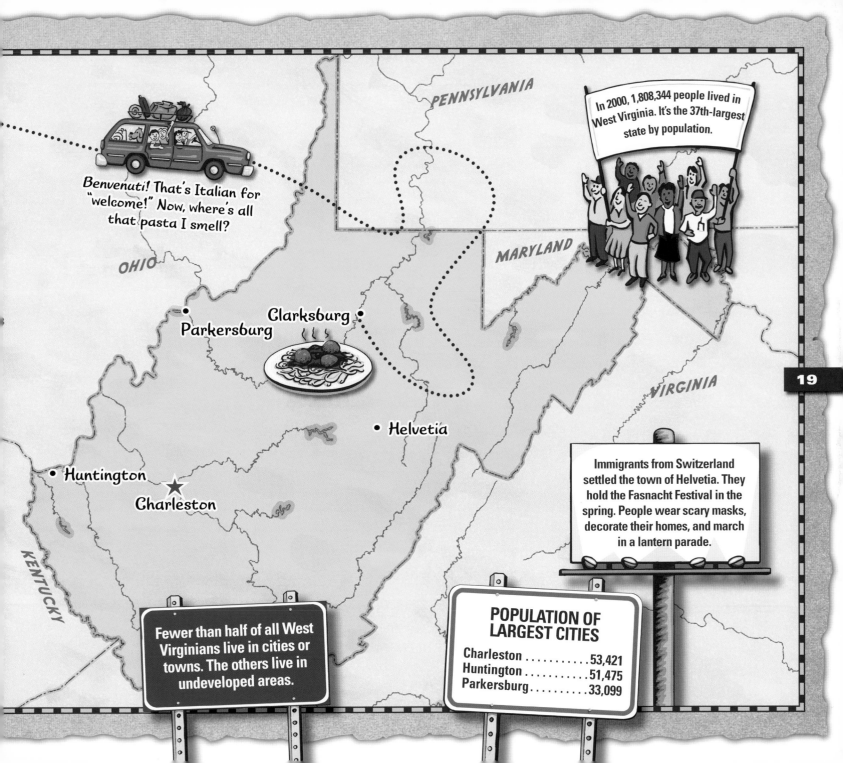

Benvenuti! That's Italian for "welcome!" Now, where's all that pasta I smell?

In 2000, 1,808,344 people lived in West Virginia. It's the 37th-largest state by population.

PENNSYLVANIA

OHIO

MARYLAND

VIRGINIA

Parkersburg

Clarksburg

Helvetia

Huntington

Charleston

KENTUCKY

Immigrants from Switzerland settled the town of Helvetia. They hold the Fasnacht Festival in the spring. People wear scary masks, decorate their homes, and march in a lantern parade.

Fewer than half of all West Virginians live in cities or towns. The others live in undeveloped areas.

POPULATION OF LARGEST CITIES

Charleston 53,421
Huntington 51,475
Parkersburg 33,099

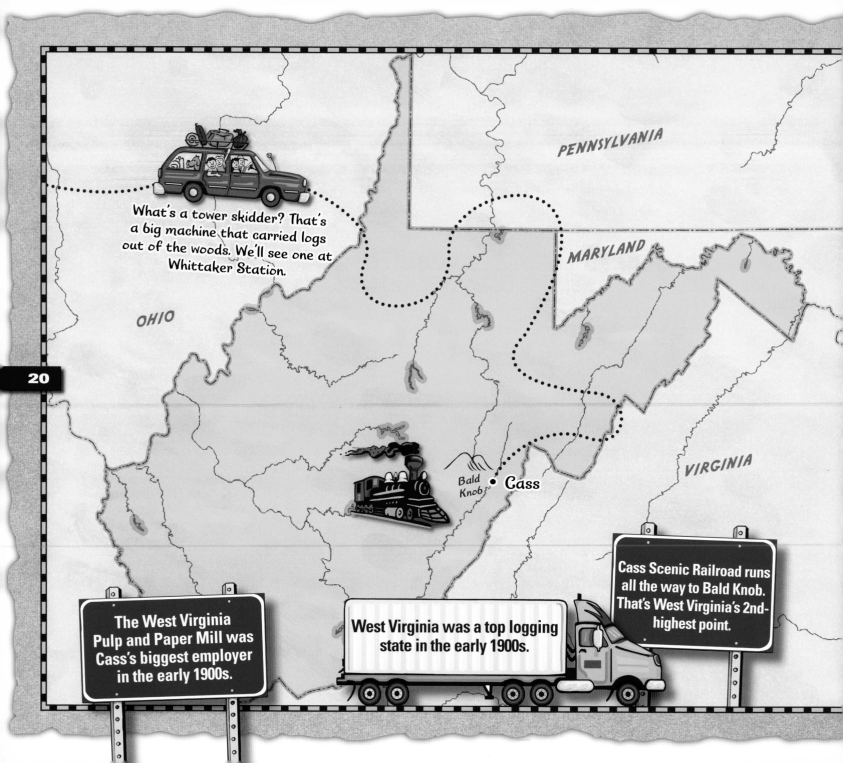

What's a tower skidder? That's a big machine that carried logs out of the woods. We'll see one at Whittaker Station.

PENNSYLVANIA

MARYLAND

OHIO

Bald Knob • Cass

VIRGINIA

The West Virginia Pulp and Paper Mill was Cass's biggest employer in the early 1900s.

West Virginia was a top logging state in the early 1900s.

Cass Scenic Railroad runs all the way to Bald Knob. That's West Virginia's 2nd-highest point.

Cass Scenic Railroad

Toot toot! All aboard! You're riding Cass Scenic Railroad. The train churns and clanks through the mountains. Thick black smoke belches from the smokestack.

At last, you get off at Whittaker Station. It's built like a 1940s logging camp. There you'll see the loggers' homes, tools, and machines.

Logging became a big industry in West Virginia. **Lumberjacks** cut down thousands of trees. Horses or trains hauled the logs away. Sawmills sawed the logs into boards. Cass was an important logging town. Most residents worked in its mills or lumber camps.

Want to ride the rails? Hop aboard a train at Cass!

Ready, set, saw! The Mountain State Forest Festival features a lumberjack contest.

The Mountain State Forest Festival in Elkins

How are your lumberjack skills? Can you chop wood or saw logs? Can you hit a target with an axe? Maybe you'd rather just watch. Then drop by the Mountain State Forest Festival!

This festival celebrates West Virginia's lumber history. It also celebrates the skills needed to survive in the forest.

Settlers made their way into the forested mountains. They worked hard to make homes there. They chopped down trees and sawed them apart. They built their houses with the logs. Sometimes they hunted with bows and arrows. They had to be tough to stay alive!

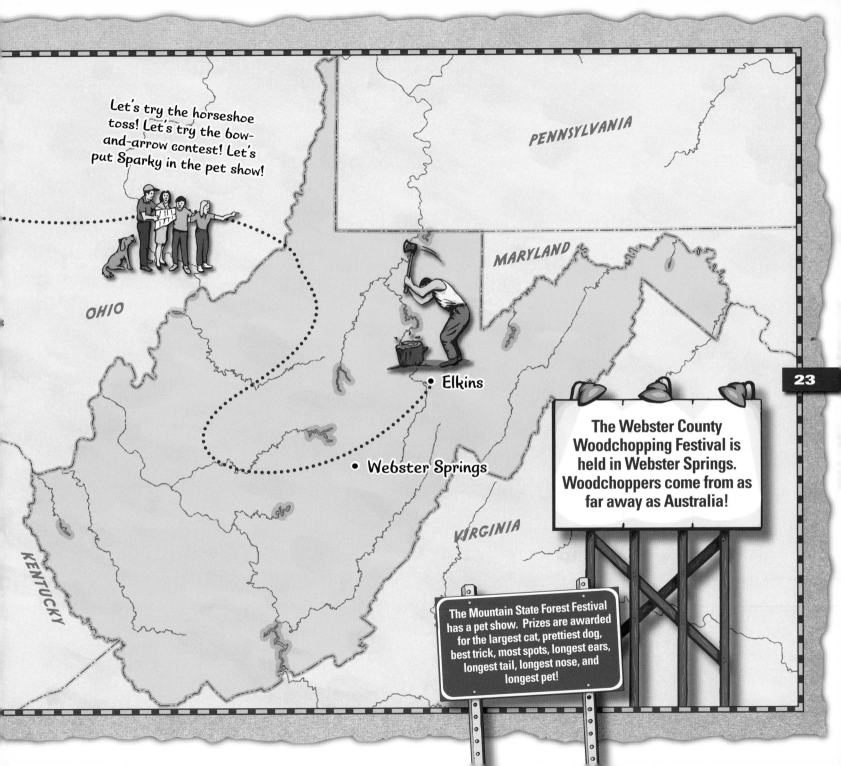

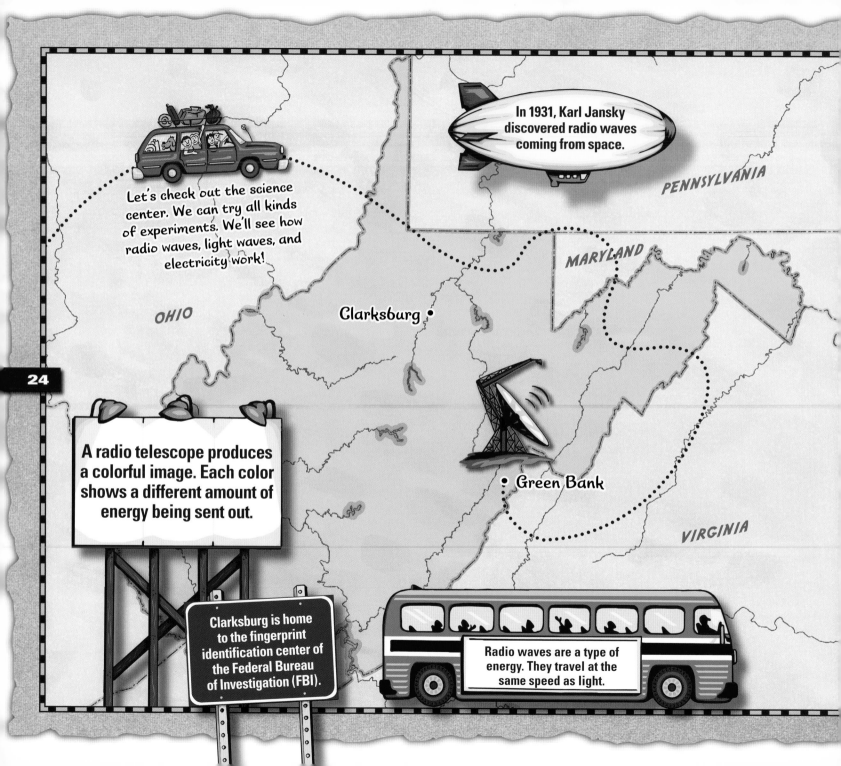

In 1931, Karl Jansky discovered radio waves coming from space.

Let's check out the science center. We can try all kinds of experiments. We'll see how radio waves, light waves, and electricity work!

PENNSYLVANIA

MARYLAND

OHIO

Clarksburg •

• Green Bank

VIRGINIA

A radio telescope produces a colorful image. Each color shows a different amount of energy being sent out.

Clarksburg is home to the fingerprint identification center of the Federal Bureau of Investigation (FBI).

Radio waves are a type of energy. They travel at the same speed as light.

The National Radio Astronomy Observatory in Green Bank

Are you curious about outer space? Do you wonder what's out there? Just visit the National Radio Astronomy Observatory (NRAO). You'll see a gigantic radio telescope. It's shaped like a big dish. Scientists at NRAO use it to study space.

What's a radio telescope? Well, a regular telescope is like your eyes. It takes in light waves. But a radio telescope takes in radio waves. Where do the radio waves come from? Objects in space give them off.

Radio telescopes "see" things that regular telescopes can't. For example, they can observe exploded stars. This helps scientists discover the secrets of the universe!

Want to learn about the universe? Check out the radio telescopes in Green Bank!

Knock, knock! Want to see the Greenbrier bunker? You have to open the steel-framed door first.

The Greenbrier bunker covers more than 112,500 square feet (10,450 sq m).

The Greenbrier Hotel in White Sulphur Springs

Stroll into the elegant Greenbrier Hotel. People have come to this location since 1778. Its hot mineral waters are very healthful.

You can come and soak in the waters, too. You can also take a strange tour. You'll visit the hotel's underground bunker, or shelter. It has a cafeteria, recreation room, and hospital. Bunk beds fill the sleeping area. People could live here for months!

That was the idea. The U.S. government built this bunker. It could be used in case of war. Members of Congress would be able to live there safely. The shelter was closed in 1995. Now it gives visitors a peek into history.

The underground cafeteria used to have paintings of pretty outdoor scenes. That would help residents forget they were underground!

PENNSYLVANIA

MARYLAND

OHIO

Berkeley Springs

VIRGINIA

Berkeley Springs is another town with springs of hot mineral water. The town holds the International Water Tasting Competition every year.

KENTUCKY

White Sulphur Springs

Construction on the Greenbrier bunker began in 1959. It was completed in 1962. The bunker was never used for its intended purpose.

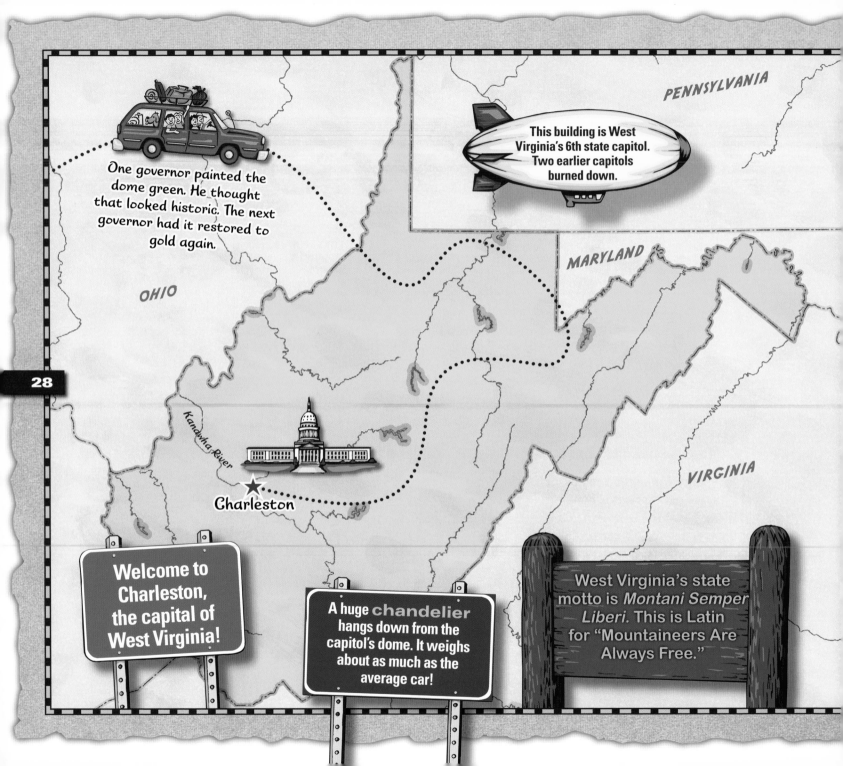

One governor painted the dome green. He thought that looked historic. The next governor had it restored to gold again.

This building is West Virginia's 6th state capitol. Two earlier capitols burned down.

PENNSYLVANIA

MARYLAND

OHIO

VIRGINIA

Kanawha River

★ Charleston

Welcome to Charleston, the capital of West Virginia!

A huge **chandelier** hangs down from the capitol's dome. It weighs about as much as the average car!

West Virginia's state motto is *Montani Semper Liberi.* This is Latin for "Mountaineers Are Always Free."

The State Capitol in Charleston

Lots of state capitols have a dome. Only a few have a *golden* dome, though. One is West Virginia's capitol. Its gold-coated dome glistens in the sunlight!

The state capitol overlooks the Kanawha River. Its shiny dome can be seen for miles.

Inside the capitol are state government offices. The state legislature meets here. It's the lawmaking branch of the state government. The governor heads another branch. Its job is to carry out the laws. Judges make up the third branch of the government. They decide whether someone has broken the law.

Lawmakers are busy inside the capitol in Charleston.

Are apples your favorite fruit? Then West Virginia's the state for you!

Golden Delicious apples were first grown in West Virginia.

The Apple Butter Festival in Berkeley Springs

Do you have a speedy turtle? Then enter it in the turtle race. Are you good at tossing eggs? How about calling hogs? You can enter contests for those skills, too.

You're at the Apple Butter Festival! Sniff the air while you're there. You'll smell old-fashioned apple butter. People at the festival make it all day.

Eastern West Virginia is a big apple-growing region. Animals are the state's top farm products, though. Chickens and beef cattle are the most valuable. Hay is West Virginia's leading crop. Most of it ends up as cattle feed.

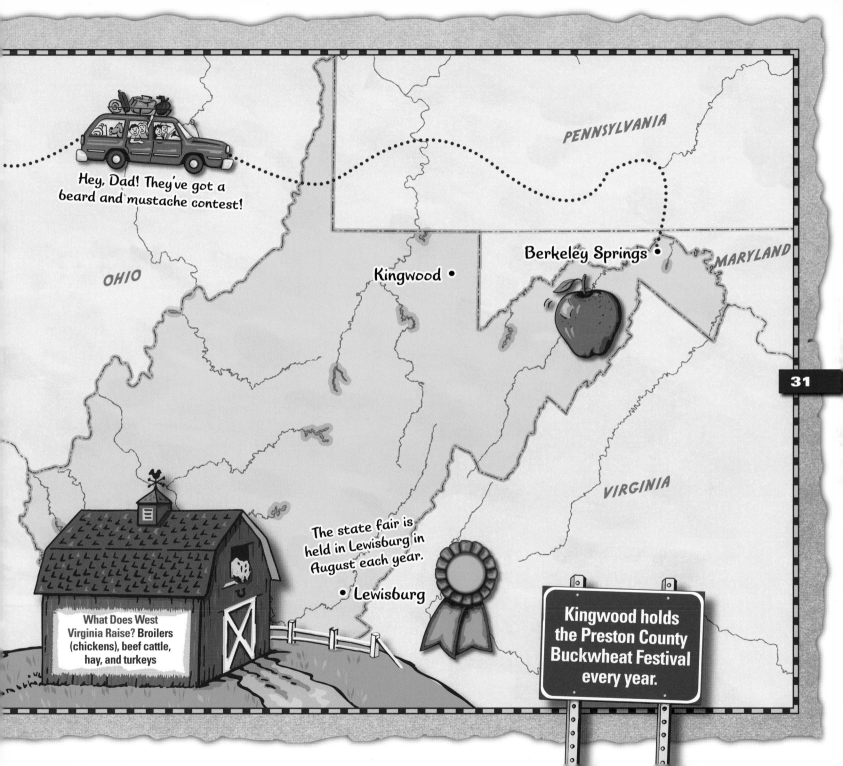

Hey, Dad! They've got a beard and mustache contest!

PENNSYLVANIA

MARYLAND

OHIO

Berkeley Springs •

Kingwood •

VIRGINIA

The state fair is held in Lewisburg in August each year.

• Lewisburg

What Does West Virginia Raise? Broilers (chickens), beef cattle, hay, and turkeys

Kingwood holds the Preston County Buckwheat Festival every year.

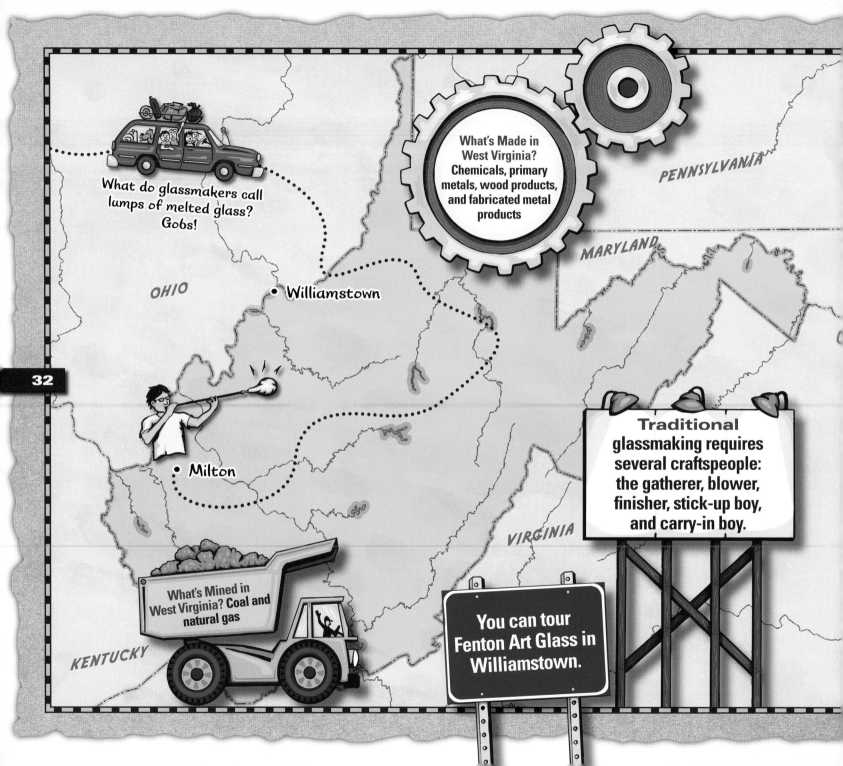

What do glassmakers call lumps of melted glass? Gobs!

What's Made in West Virginia? Chemicals, primary metals, wood products, and fabricated metal products

PENNSYLVANIA

MARYLAND

OHIO

• Williamstown

• Milton

Traditional glassmaking requires several craftspeople: the gatherer, blower, finisher, stick-up boy, and carry-in boy.

VIRGINIA

What's Mined in West Virginia? Coal and natural gas

You can tour Fenton Art Glass in Williamstown.

KENTUCKY

Blenko Glass Company in Milton

A blower makes glass at Blenko Glass Company.

A worker leans over the super-hot furnace. He gathers a gob of melted glass. The blower blows the gob into a shape. Then the finisher adds handles. Finally, there's a beautiful glass vase!

You're watching workers at Blenko Glass Company. West Virginia is famous for its glass products. Glass factories create bottles, stained glass, and windows. They make both useful and decorative glassware.

Chemicals are the state's top factory goods. Many chemicals are made from West Virginia's minerals. Those minerals include coal, natural gas, oil, and salt. Many factories also make metal or wood products.

Strike up a tune! Musicians perform at the
West Virginia State Folk Festival.

Ripley holds the
Mountain State
Art and Craft
Fair in July.

The Folk Festival in Glenville

Kick up your heels to a fiddle tune. Hear an old-timer tell a tall tale. Watch a wood-carver hand-carve a bird. Then gobble up some beans and cornbread. You're enjoying the West Virginia State Folk Festival!

This festival celebrates traditions of the Appalachian Region. People there developed many arts and crafts.

Today, the mountains are great for outdoor fun. People camp, hike, and watch wildlife there. In winter, people ski in the Allegheny Mountains. West Virginia's rivers attract lots of visitors, too. They drift downstream in kayaks or canoes. What a great escape!

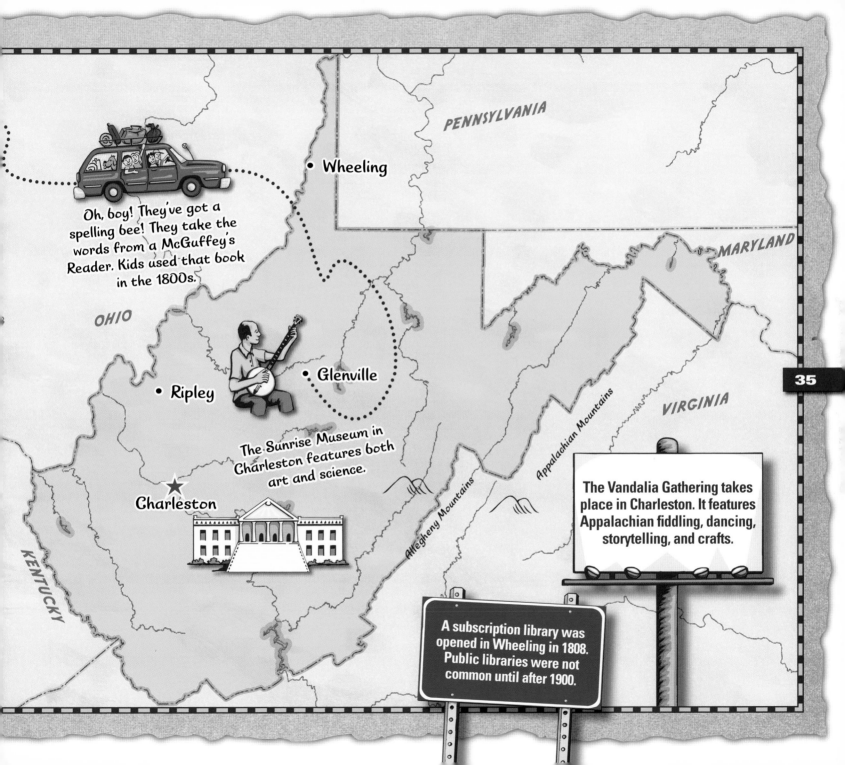

PENNSYLVANIA

• Wheeling

MARYLAND

Oh, boy! They've got a spelling bee! They take the words from a McGuffey's Reader. Kids used that book in the 1800s.

OHIO

VIRGINIA

• Ripley

• Glenville

The Sunrise Museum in Charleston features both art and science.

★ Charleston

Appalachian Mountains

Allegheny Mountains

The Vandalia Gathering takes place in Charleston. It features Appalachian fiddling, dancing, storytelling, and crafts.

KENTUCKY

A subscription library was opened in Wheeling in 1808. Public libraries were not common until after 1900.

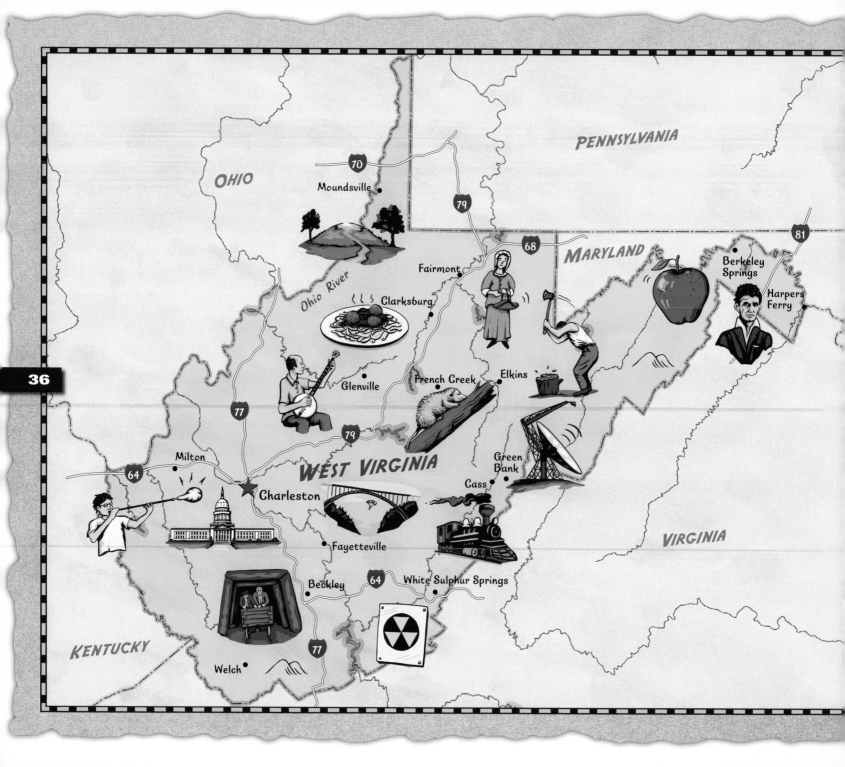

PENNSYLVANIA

OHIO

70

Moundsville

79

68

MARYLAND

81

Fairmont

Ohio River

Clarksburg

Berkeley
Springs

Harpers
Ferry

French Creek

Elkins

77

Glenville

79

Green
Bank

Milton

64

Cass

WEST VIRGINIA

Charleston

Fayetteville

VIRGINIA

Beckley

64

White Sulphur Springs

KENTUCKY

77

Welch

OUR TRIP

We visited many amazing places on our trip! We also met a lot of interesting people along the way. Look at the map on the left. Use your finger to trace all the places we have been.

What type of animal is West Virginia shaped like? See page 7 for the answer.

How big is the shell of an adult spotted turtle? Page 8 has the answer.

When did West Virginia enter the Union? Look on page 14 for the answer.

What city holds the King Coal Festival each year? See page 16 for the answer.

How far underground does Beckley Exhibition Coal Mine go? Page 17 has the answer.

What is the largest city in West Virginia? Turn to page 19 for the answer.

Where is the Webster County Woodchopping Festival held? Look on page 23 for the answer.

What type of apple was first grown in West Virginia? Turn to page 30 for the answer.

That was a great trip! We have traveled all over West Virginia!
There are a few places that we didn't have time for, though. Next time, we plan to visit the Kimball War Memorial in Welch. The memorial was built in 1928. It honors African Americans who fought bravely during World War I.

More Places to Visit in West Virginia

WORDS TO KNOW

arsenal (AR-suh-nul) a storehouse for weapons

chandelier (shan-duh-LEER) a fancy light fixture that hangs down from the ceiling

colony (KOL-uh-nee) a land with ties to a mother country

cultures (KUHL-churz) the customs, beliefs, and ways of life of groups of people

ethnic (ETH-nik) having to do with a person's race or nationality

immigrants (IM-uh-gruhnts) people who move from their home country to another country

industry (IN-duh-stree) a type of business

lumberjacks (LUM-burr-jaks) people who cut trees down and saw them into logs

pioneers (py-uh-NEERZ) people who move to an unsettled land

rappel (ruh-PELL) to descend from a high place by sliding down a rope that's partly wrapped around the body

traditional (truh-DISH-uhn-ul) following long-held customs

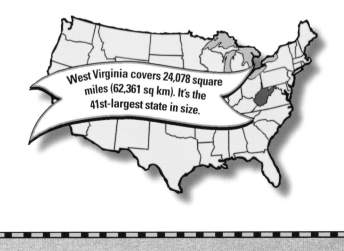

West Virginia covers 24,078 square miles (62,361 sq km). It's the 41st-largest state in size.

STATE SYMBOLS

State animal: Black bear

State bird: Cardinal

State butterfly: Monarch butterfly

State colors: Old gold and blue

State fish: Brook trout

State flower: Rhododendron (great laurel)

State fruit: Golden Delicious apple

State insect: Honeybee

State soil: Monongahela series

State tree: Sugar maple

State flag

State seal

STATE SONG

"The West Virginia Hills"

Words by Ellen King, music by H. E. Engle

Oh, the West Virginia hills!
How majestic and how grand,
With their summits bathed in glory,
Like our Prince Immanuel's land!
Is it any wonder then,
That my heart with rapture thrills,
As I stand once more with loved ones
On these West Virginia hills?

Chorus:
O the hills, Beautiful hills,
How I love those West Virginia hills.
If o'er sea or land I roam
Still I think of happy home
And the friends among the West
Virginia hills.

Oh, the West Virginia hills! Where my
childhood hours were passed,
Where I often wandered lonely, And
the future tried to cast;
Many are our visions bright, Which
the future ne'er fulfills;
But how sunny were my daydreams
On those West Virginia hills!

(Chorus)

Oh, the West Virginia hills! How
unchang'd they seem to stand,
With their summits pointed skyward T
the Great Almighty's Land!
Many changes I can see, Which my
heart with sadness fills;
But no changes can be noticed In
those West Virginia hills.

(Chorus)

Oh, the West Virginia hills! I must bi
you now adieu.
In my home beyond the mountains
shall ever dream of you;
In the evening time of life, If my Fath
only wills,
I shall still behold the vision Of thos
West Virginia hills.

(Chorus)

FAMOUS PEOPLE

Brett, George (1953–), baseball player

Buck, Pearl S. (1892–1973), author

Dru, Joanne (1922–1996), actor

Jackson, Thomas J. "Stonewall" (1824–1863), Confederate general

Knight, John S. (1894–1981), journalist and publisher

Knotts, Don (1924–), actor

Knowles, John (1926–2001), author

Marshall, Peter (1930–), actor and TV host

Martin, Christy (1968–), boxer

Nash, John Forbes, Jr. (1928–), mathematician and Nobel Prize winner

Paisley, Brad (1972–), country music singer

Retton, Mary Lou (1968–) gymnast and Olympic gold medalist

Reuther, Walter (1907–1970), labor leader

Rylant, Cynthia (1954–), children's book author

Snead, Sam (1912–2002), golfer

Vance, Cyrus (1917–2002), public official

Washington, Booker T. (1856–1915), educator and founder of the Tuskegee Institute

West, Jerry (1938–), basketball player

Woodson, Carter G. (1875–1950), educator and author

Yeager, Chuck (1923–), 1st person to fly faster than the speed of sound

TO FIND OUT MORE

At the Library

Amper, Thomas, and Jeni Reeves (illustrator). *Booker T. Washington.* Minneapolis: Carolrhoda Books, 1998.

Kent, Zachary. *The Story of John Brown's Raid on Harpers Ferry.* Chicago: Children's Press, 1988.

McKissack, Patricia, and Frederick McKissack. *Carter G. Woodson: The Father of Black History.* Berkeley Heights, N.J.: Enslow Publishers, 2002.

Riehle, Mary Ann McCabe, and Laura J. Bryant (illustrator). *M Is for Mountain State: A West Virginia Alphabet.* Chelsea, Mich.: Sleeping Bear Press, 2004.

Rylant, Cynthia, and Barry Moser (illustrator). *Appalachia: The Voices of Sleeping Birds.* San Diego: Harcourt Jovanovich, 1991.

On the Web

Visit our home page for lots of links about West Virginia: *http://www.childsworld.com/links*

Note to Parents, Teachers, and Librarians: We routinely verify our Web links to make sure they are safe, active sites—so encourage your readers to check them out!

Places to Visit or Contact

West Virginia Division of Culture and History
The Cultural Center
Capitol Complex
1900 Kanawha Boulevard East
Charleston WV 25305
304/558-0220
For more information about the history of West Virginia

West Virginia Division of Tourism and Parks
90 MacCorkle Avenue SW
South Charleston, WV 25303
304/558-2200
For more information about traveling in West Virginia

INDEX

*Bye, Mountain State.
We had a great time.
We'll come back soon!*